American Lives

Alice
Paul

Elizabeth Raum

Heinemann Library
Chicago, Illinois

© 2004 Heinemann Library
an imprint of Capstone Global Library, LLC
Chicago, Illinois

Customer Service 888-454-2279

Visit our website at www.heinemannlibrary.com

Designed by Heinemann Library
Photo research by Stephanie L. Miller
Printed and bound in the United States of
America, North Mankato, MN.

13 12 11
10 9 8 7 6 5 4 3 2

**Library of Congress Cataloging-in-Publication
Data**
Raum, Elizabeth.
  Alice Paul / Elizabeth Raum.
    v. cm. -- (American lives (Heinemann
Library (Firm)))
Includes bibliographical references and index.
Contents: A better world -- Books and tennis --
College days -- England -- Mrs. Pankhurst's
assistant -- Suffragist -- Quiet leader --
Washington's big parade -- Meeting with
president Wilson -- Arrested -- Equal rights --
Helping women everywhere -- Remembering
Miss Paul. ISBN 1-4034-4996-1 (Hardcover) --
ISBN 978-1-4034-5703-5 (Paperback) 1. Paul, Alice,
1885-1977--Juvenile literature. 2. Suffragists--
United States--Biography--Juvenile literature. 3.
Women's rights--United States--History--Juvenile
literature. [1. Paul, Alice, 1885-1977. 2. Suffragists.
3. Women's rights. 4. Women--Suffrage. 5.
Women--Biography.] I. Title. II. Series.
JK1899.P38R38 2003
324.6'23'092--dc22
052011   2003015754
006155R

Acknowledgments
The author and publishers are grateful to the
following for permission to reproduce copyright
material: Title page, pp. 4, 6, 29 Alice Paul
Institute; pp. 5, 7, 9 Courtesy of Moorestown
Friends School; p. 8 Friends Historical Library
of Swarthmore College; p. 10 New Jersey
Historical Society; pp. 11, 12, 13, 23 Hulton-
Deutsch Collection/Corbis; p. 14 Underwood
& Underwood/Corbis; pp. 16, 21 Corbis; pp. 17,
19, 22, 26 Bettmann/Corbis; p. 18 Library of
Congress; p. 20 Strong Museum, Rochester,
NY; pp. 24, 25 Stock Montage, Inc.; p. 27
Jo Freeman; p. 28 Wally McNamee/Corbis

Cover photograph by Bettmann/Corbis

The author would like to thank Lucienne M.
Beard, Program Coordinator of the Alice Paul
Centennial Foundation, for her assistance and
support with this project.

The publisher would like to thank Michelle
Rimsa for her comments in the preparation
of this book.

The cover image of Alice Paul was taken in 1926.
She was 36 years old.

Contents

Some words are shown in bold, **like this.** You can find out what they mean by looking in the glossary.

A Better World

At the time when Alice Paul was born on January 11, 1885, women could not vote. Her mother Tacie had attended Swarthmore College, a school in Pennsylvania run by people of the **Quaker** religion. Alice's father William was a banker. The Pauls believed that women should be encouraged to go to college. They believed women should have the same rights as men. They taught Alice that she could make a difference in the world.

This is a picture of Alice as a baby with her mother, Tacie, in 1885.

At home, at church, and at school, Alice learned that each person has a duty to make the world a better place. Her mother, like many Quaker women, went to meetings about women's **suffrage**, or voting rights. Alice went along to listen and learn. When she grew up, Alice spent her life helping women gain rights equal to those of men.

The Moorestown Friends Meeting House in Mt. Laurel was probably where Alice's family attended meetings.

Books and Games

The Pauls lived in Mt. Laurel, New Jersey, about fifteen miles from Philadelphia, Pennsylvania. Alice attended a **Quaker** school. She was a good student who loved to read. Her family owned lots of books, and Alice read most of them. Her favorite author was Charles Dickens, an English writer. He wrote *A Christmas Carol, Oliver Twist,* and other tales about children who were poor or treated badly.

Alice is shown here (at left) with her sister Helen and brother Billy.

When she was not reading, Alice played with her younger brothers, William and Parry, and her sister Helen. Their home had a big porch that wrapped all the way around it. In front of the porch was a huge lawn with a tennis court. When the children grew tired of playing tennis, they played checkers or other quiet games.

Alice played field hockey at Moorestown Friends School. She is the girl on the left in the front row.

College Days

Alice graduated from high school in 1901.

At age sixteen, Alice went to Swarthmore College as her mother had done. She took classes in **biology.** During her last year at college, Alice took a class in **politics.** That class helped her to understand why voting was so important.

Politics

The activities of the people in the government are called politics. American politicians are elected by the people. Voting gives people the power to change the way they live. They can elect people who will make good and fair laws.

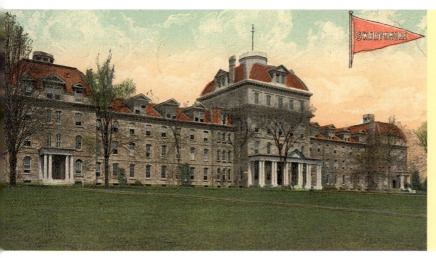

Swarthmore College was originally a school in Pennsylvania run by **Quakers.** It is still open today.

After college, Alice studied **social work** at a school in New York City. The school later became part of Columbia University. She joined **social workers** helping poor people. Alice admired the social workers, but she did not want to help just one family at a time. She wanted to do something that improved the way everyone lived. In the fall of 1906, Alice moved to Philadelphia to continue her studies at the University of Pennsylvania. She wrote a paper on the rights of women in Pennsylvania.

England

In 1907, Alice won a **scholarship** to study at a **Quaker** school in England. While in England, she met another young American named Lucy Burns. Lucy became a lifelong friend and later worked with Alice on women's **suffrage.**

Before Alice began her studies, she went on a bicycle trip through France with some friends. When she returned to London, she studied **economics** and **social work.**

Alice was determined to fight for the rights of women everywhere.

The Life of Alice Paul

1885	1905	1907	1913	1917	1920
Born on January 11 in Mt. Laurel, New Jersey	*Graduated from Swarthmore College*	*Moved to England*	*Led March on Washington*	*Arrested and jailed*	*Women win the vote*

While Alice was in England, she went to hear a young lawyer named Christabel Pankhurst talk about voting rights for women. The audience did not believe in giving women the vote, so they yelled and shouted during her speech. School officials had to cancel the event. Alice admired Pankhurst's courage and agreed with her ideas. She decided to help Pankhurst and the other London women fighting for women's suffrage.

In this 1912 photo, Pankhurst holds a newspaper with the headline "Votes for Women."

1922	1923	1945	1964	1977
Earned law degree	*Wrote Equal Rights Amendment*	*Fought to include rights for women in United Nations Charter*	*Worked to include women in Civil Rights Act*	*Died on July 9 in Moorestown*

Mrs. Pankhurst's Assistant

Alice and her friend Lucy attended political meetings with Christabel Pankhurst and Pankhurst's mother, who was a **suffrage** leader. They shouted, "Votes for women!" Pankhurst asked Alice to work with her. Alice marched in a big parade through London and spoke about women's suffrage on street corners. Pankhurst and her followers were willing to go to jail if that would help convince the government to give voting rights to women.

The Suffragette Parade took place on June 19, 1911, in Trafalger Square in London, England.

Alice was arrested ten times and sent to jail three times while she was in England. She and the other women were charged with disturbing the peace. Newspaper stories about the arrests drew even more attention to the fight for voting rights.

By the time Alice returned home, news of her work with Pankhurst had reached the United States. Members of the National American Woman Suffrage Association (NAWSA) asked Alice to join them.

Alice took a ship home from England. This photo was taken aboard the ship.

Marching for Votes

In 1910, in Washington, Alice gave a speech about her **suffrage** work in England. In 1912, Philadelphia **suffragists** asked Alice to be in charge of a committee that planned parades and other events. The group was called the Congressional Committee. Alice, whom everyone called Miss Paul, spoke on street corners and taught the women to **picket** for suffrage by carrying signs and banners.

Suffragettes walk down Bedford Avenue in Brooklyn, New York, to ask for votes for women.

Paul felt that the time was right for women's suffrage in the United States. Several western states had already given women the vote. If women could vote in some states, Paul asked, then why not everywhere? She and the other suffragists tried to convince women who already had the vote to elect candidates who supported the idea of suffrage for all women.

Getting the vote

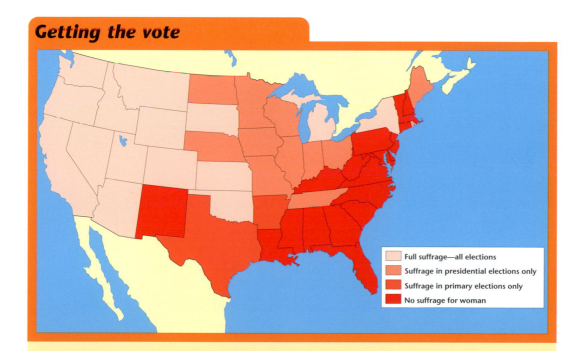

Full suffrage—all elections

Suffrage in presidential elections only

Suffrage in primary elections only

No suffrage for woman

Before the Nineteenth Amendment passed, women could only vote in a few states.

Quiet but Strong

In 1913, Paul graduated from college. She knew she wanted to make a difference.

Alice Paul did not look like a powerful leader. She was small and thin and never drew attention to herself. She listened patiently to people who disagreed with her and then calmly explained why women should vote. She was a quiet but determined leader.

Paul traveled around the country speaking about **suffrage.** She also continued to write about the need for equal rights for men and women.

Paul supported the Nineteenth **Amendment** to the U.S. Constitution. This amendment would change the Constitution to allow women to vote. It was also called the Susan B. Anthony Amendment. But many men and women still opposed

Paul (right) is shown here with other suffragettes in New York.

women's suffrage. Paul knew she would have to convince the new president, Woodrow Wilson, to support voting rights for women.

Susan B. Anthony

Susan B. Anthony was one of Alice Paul's heroes. Anthony and Elizabeth Cady Stanton started the National Woman Suffrage Association in 1869.

Washington's Big Parade

On March 3, 1913, the day before Woodrow Wilson was sworn in as president, Paul held a huge parade in Washington, D.C. She hoped to convince the new president to give women the vote. Half a million people watched the **suffrage** parade. There were 26 floats, 10 bands, 6 chariots, and about 8,000 women marching for suffrage. Women came from all over the country and from other countries to march for voting rights.

This picture shows the suffragette parade in Washington, D.C., on March 13, 1913.

The suffragettes were determined to be heard. They carried their message through the streets of Washington, D.C.

When President Wilson arrived in Washington, there was no one left to greet him. Everyone was at the suffrage parade. Some men who were against women voting attacked the marchers. Over 200 people were injured. Newspapers all over the country reported what had happened. The march drew attention to voting rights for women.

On March 17, 1913, President Wilson met with Alice Paul and a small group of **suffragists.** They urged the president to support the Nineteenth **Amendment.** The president was polite, but not very interested. The suffragists also met with members of Congress.

The women sent suffragist valentines to congressmen to remind them about their cause.

Paul decided to have more gatherings and parades. She and the suffragists spoke at political **rallies.** In 1914, Paul formed the Congressional Union for Woman Suffrage.

20

In 1915, Alice Paul and Jane Addams, who helped poor people in Chicago, formed the Women's International League for Peace and Freedom. There was a war going on in Europe. Paul told President Wilson that if women could vote, they would vote for peace.

Suffrage Worldwide

New Zealand gave women suffrage in 1893. Women could vote in Australia in 1902, in Finland in 1906, and in Norway in 1913. Women in the United States could not vote until after World War I—which was from 1914 to 1918.

Arrested

In 1916, Alice Paul formed a political group called the National Woman's Party. In January 1917, Paul led **suffragists** to **picket** in front of the White House.

The women marched slowly before the White House gates so that everyone who passed would see their purple, white, and gold banners. Over 1,000 women from across the country took turns marching day and night, winter and summer, and on every day of the week except for Sundays.

Women picketed in front of the White House for over a year and a half!

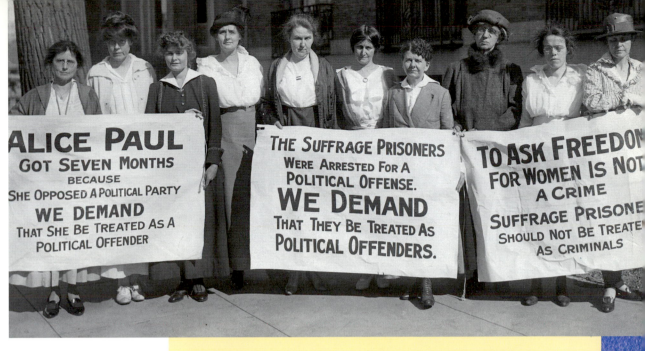

Suffragists protested the arrests of Paul and other women in their group.

After several months, the police arrested the women on charges of blocking traffic. Paul was arrested in October 1917. She was sentenced to seven months in prison. The suffragists were treated very badly in prison.

To protest their harsh treatment, Paul refused to eat for three weeks. She had to be forced. The guards, hoping to end her hunger strike, did not allow her to have visitors or to get mail or messages. Paul and the other suffragists were all released from prison at the end of November.

Equal Rights

Alice Paul and other suffragists gathered to celebrate winning the right to vote.

On January 9, 1918, President Wilson agreed to support women's **suffrage.** The next day, the Nineteenth **Amendment** passed in the House of Representatives by one vote! It then went to the states to be **ratified** by them.

For the next seventeen months, **suffragists** kept **picketing,** giving speeches, and getting arrested for their cause. Finally, on August 26, 1920, the state of Tennessee gave the last vote needed in the Senate to make the Nineteenth Amendment a law.

Paul wanted to be sure that women and men had equal rights. She returned to school to study law. In 1922 she became a lawyer.

Once women could vote, Paul wrote an amendment to the Constitution called the Equal Rights Amendment (ERA). The ERA says that no one can be denied equal rights because of being female. Paul wanted women to have all the same **opportunities** as men. The ERA was sent to Congress in 1923.

Although women now had the right to vote, Paul knew there were more battles to be fought for women's rights.

Helping Women Everywhere

The ERA did not pass in 1923, but Alice Paul did not give up. In 1927 and 1928 she earned two more law degrees, which helped her as she continued to work for passage of the Equal Rights **Amendment** in the United States. During the 1920s, Paul also spent time in Europe and in Latin America working for peace and women's rights. In 1938 she started the World Woman's Party. Its **headquarters** were in Switzerland.

Paul used the radio to tell others about the new headquarters for the National Women's Party in Washington, D.C.

Paul lived in Washington, D.C., whenever she was not working in other countries. She believed if women had more of a voice in **politics,** many problems could be solved. In 1945 she insisted that the United Nations include equal rights in its **charter**. Thanks to Paul's efforts, the United Nations supports the worth of every human person. They support equal rights for men and women throughout the world.

This banner shows the wording of the Equal Rights Amendment passed by Congress in 1972.

Remembering Alice Paul

Paul's work for women's rights never stopped. She is shown here at age 85.

Paul never stopped working for equal rights for women. She gave speeches, wrote letters, and worked with women's groups during the 1950s and 1960s to push the ERA forward.

She also made sure that women's rights were included in the 1964 Civil Rights Act. The Act protected the rights of all Americans, regardless of race or color. When she got older, Paul moved to Connecticut.

ALICE PAUL INSTITUTE

The Alice Paul Institute was created in 1984 to celebrate 100 years since Paul's birth. It is in Mt. Laurel, New Jersey.

Paul finished out her life in a nursing home in Moorestown, New Jersey. She died on July 9, 1977, at age 92. On August 26, 1977, women's groups held a march in Washington. They marched in honor of Paul and her life's work toward improving the rights of women.

The ERA never got enough votes to become a law. But thanks to Alice Paul, people around the world continue to discuss the importance of equal rights for all people.

Glossary

amendment change made in a bill or law

biology science that deals with living things

charter paper stating the aims of an organization like the United Nations

economics study of how people make and use money, goods, and services

headquarters main office

opportunity good chance

passage vote making something into a law

picket to stand outside a building for a period of time to protest something

politics activities of people in government

Quaker Christian group which began in England; also called the Society of Friends

rally meeting for a special purpose

ratify approve

scholarship gift of money to pay for school

social work service to help a person or group

social worker person who earns a living by doing social work

suffrage right to vote

suffragist person who believes in women's right to vote

More Books to Read

Keller, Kristin Thoennes. *The Women Suffrage Movement, 1848-1920*. Mankato, Minn.: Bridgestone, 2003.

Pascoe, Elaine. *The Right to Vote*. Brooklyn, N.Y.: Millbrook Press, 1997.

Places to Visit

Paulsdale

(birthplace and home of Alice Paul)

128 Hooton Road

Mount Laurel, New Jersey 08054

Visitor Information: (856) 231-1885

Sewall-Belmont House

(home of the National Woman's Party)

144 Constitution Avenue, NE

Washington, D.C. 20002-5608

Visitor Information: (202) 546-1210

Index